A HISTORY OF

PAPERBIRD

Acknowledgments:
The author and publishers would like to thank Mr Mike Gibson for his help in research, and the following for permission to use illustrative material:
Cover and page 51 (top): T. N. Birkinshaw; 48: Bridgeman Art Library; cover and 36 (2): City of Kingston upon Hull Museums and Art Galleries; 9: Eilean Donan Castle; 13 (top right): Institute of Agricultural History and Museum of English Rural Life, University of Reading; 46: A. F. Kersting; 34/35 (bottom): The Mansell Collection; cover and 45 (3): National Maritime Museum; 6 (2), 7 (2), 8, 13 (centre and top right), 14, 17 (top right), 22 (bottom), 28, 34 (top left): National Portrait Gallery, London; 17 (centre), 49: Royal Armouries Board of Trustees; 31: courtesy of the Royal College of Surgeons, Edinburgh; 19, 21, 22 (top), 51: Science Museum, London; illustrations on pages 33 and 40 by Pete Storey; cover and background photograph: Woodmansterne Picture Library; 38: by courtesy of the Wedgwood Museum Trustees, Barlaston, Stoke-on-Trent; illustration on page 10 by Gavin Young (reference from Smuggling on Wight Island, with thanks to Mr Dowling).
Designed by Gavin Young.

British Library Cataloguing in Publication Data

Wood, Tim
    The Georgians. — (A History of Britain)
    1. Great Britain, 1714 – 1837
    I. Title   II. Dillow, John   III. Series
    941.07

    ISBN 1-85543-011-8

First edition

Published by Ladybird Books Ltd Loughborough Leicestershire UK
Ladybird Books Inc Auburn Maine 04210 USA
Paperbird is an imprint of Ladybird Books Ltd
© LADYBIRD BOOKS LTD MCMXCI

Printed in England (3)

Contents

The Georgians

by TIM WOOD

illustrations by JOHN DILLOW

Series Consultants: School of History
University of Bristol

Paperbird

The Georgians

This book covers a period of over a hundred years, from 1714 to 1830. This time is known as the Georgian Period, because the four kings who ruled Britain were all named George. During these years the chief *ministers* of Parliament became more powerful while the king became less important. Life for most people changed with the growth of towns and the start of the *Industrial Revolution*.

Britain and the British Empire during the Georgian Period

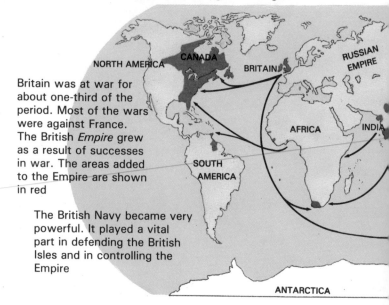

Britain was at war for about one-third of the period. Most of the wars were against France. The British *Empire* grew as a result of successes in war. The areas added to the Empire are shown in red

The British Navy became very powerful. It played a vital part in defending the British Isles and in controlling the Empire

Events during Georgian Period

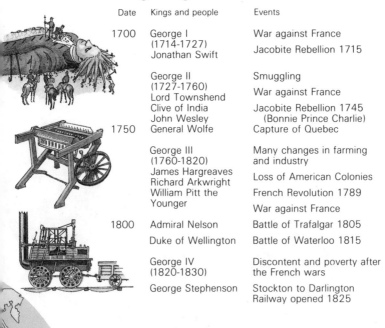

Date	Kings and people	Events
1700	George I (1714-1727) Jonathan Swift	War against France Jacobite Rebellion 1715
	George II (1727-1760) Lord Townshend Clive of India John Wesley	Smuggling War against France Jacobite Rebellion 1745 (Bonnie Prince Charlie)
1750	General Wolfe	Capture of Quebec
	George III (1760-1820) James Hargreaves Richard Arkwright William Pitt the Younger	Many changes in farming and industry Loss of American Colonies French Revolution 1789 War against France
1800	Admiral Nelson	Battle of Trafalgar 1805
	Duke of Wellington	Battle of Waterloo 1815
	George IV (1820-1830)	Discontent and poverty after the French wars
	George Stephenson	Stockton to Darlington Railway opened 1825

JAPAN

CHINA

AUSTRALIA

NEW
ZEALAND

Britain was already an important manufacturing country at the start of the period, but most of the work was done by hand. During the Georgian Period Britain became the most important manufacturing country in the world as a result of the invention of machines powered by water and steam.

The four Georges

Queen Anne had no children that lived, so when she died in 1714 Parliament offered the crown to a German prince, George of Hanover, the great-grandson of James I. He became George I. George I and the three King Georges who followed him were unpopular for large parts of their reigns.

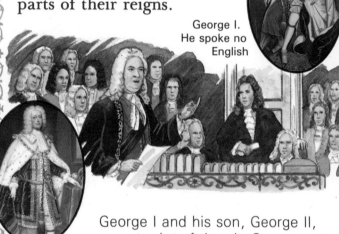

George I.
He spoke no
English

George II

George I and his son, George II, spent a lot of time in Germany and allowed a *cabinet* of powerful MPs (Members of Parliament) to take most of the decisions for them. This group was led for many years by Sir Robert Walpole, who became Britain's first Prime Minister.

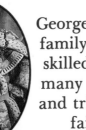

George III. He was called 'Farmer George'

George III was a good family man but was not skilled at politics. He felt many MPs were dishonest and tried to rule more fairly by building up a party of friends in Parliament. He was not however very successful and during his reign Britain lost the American colonies. George was interested in farming and encouraged many improvements in agriculture. During the later years of his reign he went mad.

George IV. This is how cartoonists of the day drew him. He led a very wild life and was mainly interested in enjoying himself. His behaviour made him very unpopular with the British people.

Bonnie Prince Charlie

Bonnie Prince
Charlie

The battle of Culloden.
The wild Highlanders
were no match for the
well-armed English army

Prince Charles Edward was the
handsome, ambitious grandson of
James II, known as Bonnie Prince Charlie.
He believed that the crown should be
returned to the Stuarts. In 1745 he
landed in Scotland with French support
to raise an army among the *clans* and
gain the throne. After an early victory

at the battle of Prestonpans, he invaded England.

When he found that few English people supported him, Charles retreated, going back to the Highlands of Scotland. He was pursued by George II's son, the Duke of Cumberland. At Culloden, near Inverness, the tired clansmen were at last defeated. A reward of £30,000 was put on Charles' head, but he hid and later escaped abroad.

Charles was helped to escape by Flora Macdonald

A lock of Bonnie Prince Charlie's hair kept in Eilean Donan castle

'Butcher' Cumberland and his soldiers hunted down the rebels or Jacobites. Many were killed or transported abroad

Trade and smuggling

During Georgian times British ships traded all over the world. They carried industrial goods to Europe, the Americas and India, and brought back luxuries like silk, sugar, tea, brandy and tobacco. Many people, especially along the south coast, turned to smuggling to avoid paying the high taxes on these expensive luxuries.

Smugglers however could be hanged or transported if they were caught by Customs men.

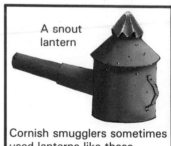

A snout lantern

Cornish smugglers sometimes used lanterns like these

Smugglers, who were often fishermen, took cargoes from foreign ships, then brought them ashore secretly. Cargoes were hidden until they could be safely sold, often to merchants and shopkeepers in the big cities.

Fine lace like this was prized by the smugglers

Barrels of brandy might be towed behind the smuggling boat. If it was stopped the barrels would sink out of sight. Many smuggling boats had false bottoms where the cargo could be hidden and then covered with fish.

Shipwrecks were looted and sometimes whole villages shared in the profits from the stolen goods.

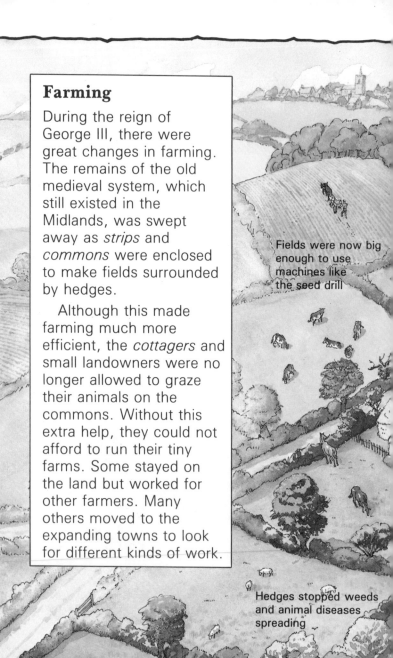

Farming

During the reign of George III, there were great changes in farming. The remains of the old medieval system, which still existed in the Midlands, was swept away as *strips* and *commons* were enclosed to make fields surrounded by hedges.

Although this made farming much more efficient, the *cottagers* and small landowners were no longer allowed to graze their animals on the commons. Without this extra help, they could not afford to run their tiny farms. Some stayed on the land but worked for other farmers. Many others moved to the expanding towns to look for different kinds of work.

Fields were now big enough to use machines like the seed drill

Hedges stopped weeds and animal diseases spreading

Robert Bakewell showed how animals could be bred scientifically to make them bigger and heavier

Jethro Tull invented a seed drill which sowed seeds in straight lines, making crops easier to weed

New crops like turnips cleaned the soil and kept it fertile

Lord Townshend showed how farmers could get more out of their land by changing the crops each year

Barns for storing winter fodder meant that animals no longer had to be killed in the autumn

Fields were used to grow different crops each year so that they no longer had to remain *fallow* for a year

Food production increased so much that the population, which doubled during the period, could still be fed

Wolfe and Quebec

In 1756, during the reign of George II, war broke out with the French in Canada. Both sides wanted to control the land and the rich fur trade there. As long as the French occupied the powerful fortress of Quebec, they threatened the British colonies in America.

1 General James Wolfe was sent to capture the fortress of Quebec.

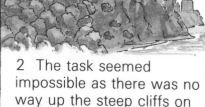

2 The task seemed impossible as there was no way up the steep cliffs on which Quebec stood.

3 Wolfe spotted a narrow path leading up to the plain behind the city and led his soldiers up it.

4 The whole British army crept up the narrow path to the Heights of Abraham behind Quebec during the night. They tricked the enemy sentries by answering their challenges in French.

5 Seeing the British in position, the French General Montcalm led out his soldiers.

6 The British waited until the French were very close, then fired. The French were beaten, but Wolfe was killed in the battle.

7 Quebec surrendered and Canada became a British colony.

The loss of America

The Boston Tea Party, 1773. Some colonists, dressed as Indians, threw tea into Boston harbour as a protest against high tea taxes

During the reign of George III the thirteen British colonies in America declared their independence from Britain. The *colonists* hated paying new taxes on goods like sugar, tea and paper. Many Americans felt no loyalty to a king who was 4,800 kilometres (3,000 miles) away and never visited America.

George Washington, victorious
general and first President
of the USA

Although George III sent
an army to put down the
rebellion, the Americans, led
by George Washington and
helped by the French, eventually forced
the British to surrender at Yorktown in
1781. A new country, the United States
of America, was born with
Washington as its first
President.

A British
'Brown Bess'
musket

The coming of machines

During the Georgian Period trade, industry and towns, especially in the north of England and the Midlands, became much more important. This change, now called the Industrial Revolution, slowly altered the appearance of the country, as well as the ways in which people lived and worked.

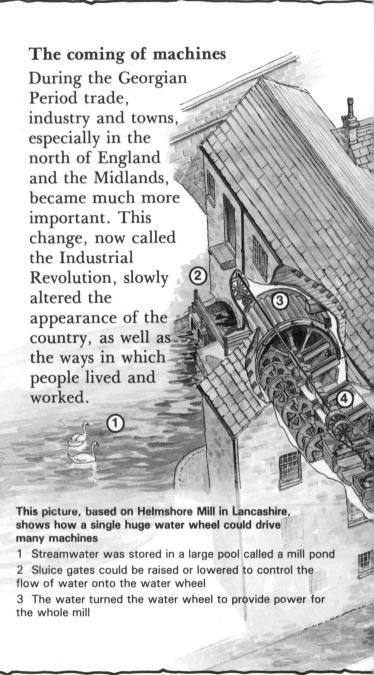

This picture, based on Helmshore Mill in Lancashire, shows how a single huge water wheel could drive many machines

1 Streamwater was stored in a large pool called a mill pond

2 Sluice gates could be raised or lowered to control the flow of water onto the water wheel

3 The water turned the water wheel to provide power for the whole mill

The main change that took place was a result of the invention of machines to do work that used to be done by hand, as in the cloth making industry. These machines, driven at first by water and later by steam, were so large that they had to be put into special buildings. This meant that many cloth workers started to work in factories instead of at home.

Richard Arkwright, a Preston barber, invented the water frame spinning machine and built one of the factories. He left over half a million pounds when he died.

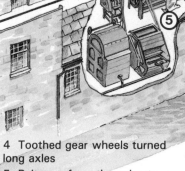

4 Toothed gear wheels turned long axles

5 Belts ran from the axles to drive the *fulling* machines as well as the spinning and weaving machines which were added later

James Hargreaves invented the Spinning Jenny after watching his wife at her spinning wheel

Iron and coal

As the Industrial Revolution got under way, more iron of a better quality was needed. For

Charcoal making. Wood was baked in an earth mound

centuries iron *smelting* had been done with charcoal, but as wood became scarce, iron makers began to use coal instead. It was Abraham Darby who showed how coal baked into coke could be used to smelt iron.

A blast furnace for smelting iron by coke

The dangers miners faced

Sparks from the pickaxe or the candle flame could set off explosive gas

Wooden pit props held up the roof

Young women dragged the coal along the tunnels

Children sat for hours in the dark waiting to open the trap doors

Coal was already used to heat homes, and in the brick making and beer brewing industries. Since most of the coal near the surface had been used up, miners had to dig much deeper to get the extra coal needed for the growing population and the new industries.

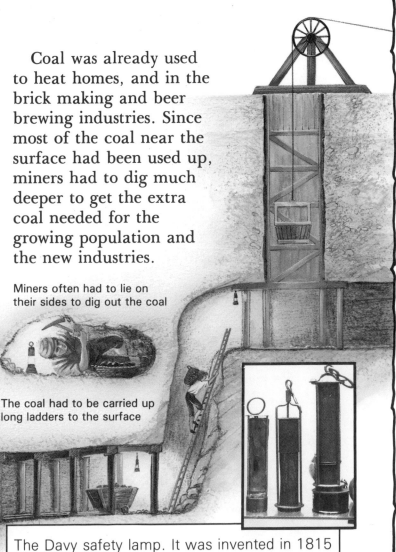

Miners often had to lie on their sides to dig out the coal

The coal had to be carried up long ladders to the surface

The Davy safety lamp. It was invented in 1815 and called 'the miners' friend' because it gave them enough light to see by, but was not hot enough to explode any gas.

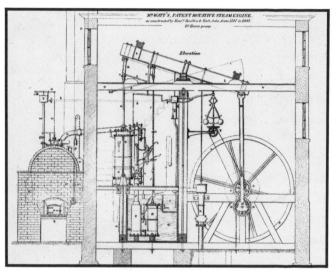

One of Watt's original steam engines

The steam engine

Probably the single most important invention of the Industrial Revolution was the steam engine. Steam engines were much more powerful and reliable than water wheels which did not work if the river dried up in hot weather or froze in winter.

James Watt. He was a scientific instrument maker at Glasgow University. While repairing a steam engine built by another inventor, he realised that there were a number of improvements he could make to it.

The first efficient steam engine was built in 1769 by James Watt. He went into partnership with a Birmingham businessman, Matthew Boulton, whose factory at Soho, near Birmingham, made hundreds of improved steam engines to Watt's new design.

Some uses of steam power

To pump floodwater out of mines

To drive the machines in the factories of the north and the Midlands

Steam powered ships. The *Charlotte Dundas* launched in 1802

Steam engines on wheels became the first railway locomotives.

George Stephenson's *Rocket*, built in 1829

Canals

In 1759, the Duke of Bridgewater paid an engineer called James Brindley to build a canal for him. The Duke had a coal mine on his estate at Worsley. He wanted the canal so that he could send his coal by barge to be sold in Manchester, eleven kilometres (seven miles) away.

This was a very efficient way of moving heavy loads. One horse could pull a barge

◄ Barton Aqueduct

containing the loads of over sixty packhorses. The canal was so successful that others were soon built to link the industrial areas of the north and the Midlands with London and the big ports.

Brindley, who could neither read nor write, finished the project in two years. He built the magnificent Barton *Aqueduct* to carry the canal over the River Irwell.

Where canals had to go up or down hills, the engineers built locks or tunnels

lock

legging a barge through a tunnel

Josiah Wedgwood owned pottery factories in Stoke-on-Trent. He realised that his delicate pottery could be carried much more safely by canal than it could on bumpy roads. He paid Brindley to build another canal from Stoke to the port of Liverpool.

Crime and punishment

Crime was very common in Georgian Britain. In the rapidly growing towns, and especially in London, hordes of poor people, beggars and ruffians lived off crime. There was no proper police force so there were savage punishments for those who were caught, to put others off committing crimes.

The pillory was used for rogues and cheats who were often pelted by the crowd

In 1750 Henry Fielding set up the first detective force, later known as the Bow Street Runners. His blind brother, John, was a *magistrate*, who was said to be able to recognise the voice of any criminal who had appeared before him.

There were over two hundred crimes for which the penalty was death. Huge crowds went to see public hangings like the ones at Tyburn, just outside London. There were often stalls and side shows as well.

Prisons were dirty and overcrowded. Murderers, lunatics, debtors and children were all mixed together in dreadful conditions. Typhus, or 'jail fever', killed a lot of prisoners each year. Some people, like John Howard, a magistrate, tried to improve conditions, but it took over fifty years to replace all the old, unhealthy prisons.

A prison hulk. Many convicted criminals were kept in old ships like these before being transported to prison camps in Australia.

John Wesley

During the Georgian Period many clergymen thought more about their own daily duties than about bringing new people to the church. Often there were no churches in the pit villages and the new industrial towns of the north. John Wesley decided to take religion to the working people.

Wesley had been a clergyman in the Church of England but came to believe that many church people were lazy and pleasure-loving

Wesley travelled thousands of kilometres round the country on horseback, preaching over forty thousand sermons in the open air, often to vast crowds. His followers were known as Methodists because they had a strict method of study and prayer, although they always worshipped with joy and enthusiasm. By the time Wesley died in 1791, a new faith had been planted in Britain.

Some clergymen grew angry when they saw how popular Wesley had become. Sometimes they encouraged ruffians to break up Methodist meetings.

John's brother Charles wrote over six thousand five hundred famous hymns.

Love divine all loves excelling
Joy of Heaven to Earth come down,
Fix in us thy humble dwelling,
All thy faithful mercies crown.

Medicine

During the Georgian Period the population of Britain more than doubled. This was partly because people married earlier and had more children, and partly because doctors were beginning to understand the human body and to learn more about how to treat some diseases.

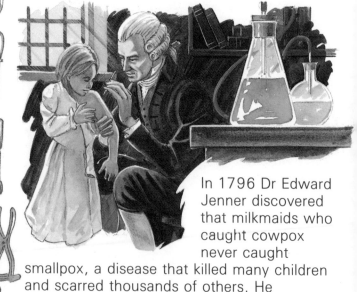

In 1796 Dr Edward Jenner discovered that milkmaids who caught cowpox never caught smallpox, a disease that killed many children and scarred thousands of others. He *vaccinated* people with a mild dose of cowpox which protected them from the killer disease.

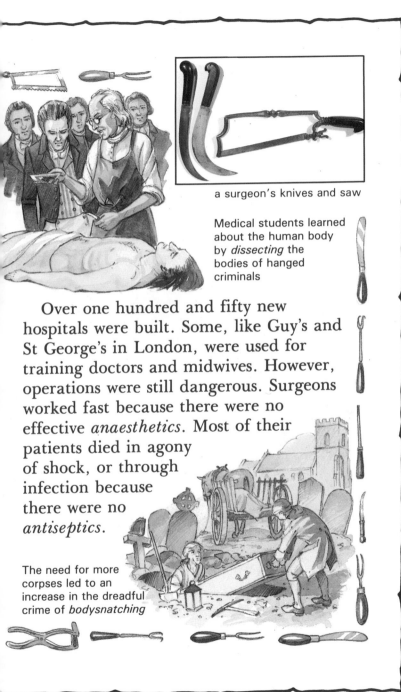

a surgeon's knives and saw

Medical students learned about the human body by *dissecting* the bodies of hanged criminals

Over one hundred and fifty new hospitals were built. Some, like Guy's and St George's in London, were used for training doctors and midwives. However, operations were still dangerous. Surgeons worked fast because there were no effective *anaesthetics*. Most of their patients died in agony of shock, or through infection because there were no *antiseptics*.

The need for more corpses led to an increase in the dreadful crime of *bodysnatching*

What people ate

For poorer people food was very plain. Bread made from rye or barley was commonly eaten with cheese or butter, though white bread made from wheat flour was becoming more popular. Cheap meat was made into a broth.

The rich often dined rather too well. A churchman, Parson Woodforde, described in his diary a dinner party where he tucked into a leg of mutton with caper sauce, a pig's face, a neck of pork roasted with gooseberries, partridge, roast swan and plum pudding. Many Georgian gentlemen were overweight and suffered from *gout*!

A picture of the time showing the evils of gin

Vegetables like carrots, parsnips and cauliflowers were eaten. For the first time tea and sugar became cheap enough for most people to enjoy in small amounts. The rich ate many different kinds of meat, especially beef and mutton, as well as fish and game. They also drank fine wines, but ale was the main drink of the poor.

A still for making gin. During the period 1720 to 1750 gin drinking became very popular. Gin was very cheap, advertised as 'Drunk for a penny, dead drunk for twopence.' It was also dangerous, since it could cause blindness, madness and even death.

Captain Cook

Cook's ship the *Endeavour*

Captain Cook and Australia

Captain James Cook was one of Britain's greatest sailors. He was given command of three great voyages of exploration round the world and visited many lands that no European had ever seen before. He took scientists with him so that they could study new plants and animals.

Cook persuaded his sailors to eat pickled cabbage. As a result none of them caught *scurvy*, a disease that usually killed many sailors on long voyages.

Cook visited New Zealand and was the first European to land on the coast of Eastern Australia. He called the landing spot 'Botany Bay' because there were so many plants and animals there. Cook was killed by Hawaiians in 1779 over an argument about a stolen boat.

After 1788 Botany Bay became a prison settlement and shiploads of *convicts* were sent there. Settlers soon followed to set up farms. This threatened the way of life of the Australian *aborigines* who lived by hunting.

The slave trade

The owners of sugar plantations in the West Indies, and tobacco and cotton farms in America wanted workers. British merchants soon found that they could make huge profits by carrying slaves from Africa to America.

America
The slaves were *auctioned* and taken away by their new owners. They were usually very badly treated

This diagram shows how tightly slaves were packed on a slave ship

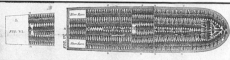

The West Indies
Ships were loaded with sugar, *molasses* and rum which fetched very high prices in Britain

3 **The West Indies**

A seal used by abolitionists. Its powerful message persuaded many Christians to support *abolition*, but it was many years before countries other than Britain stopped slavery.

slave chains

The slave triangle

1 Britain
Ships were loaded with cheap goods like beads, knives, cloth, pots and pans in ports like Liverpool and Bristol to pay for the slaves

The middle passage
The slaves were *branded*, packed onto the ships and chained in the holds. Many died on the long voyage west from disease or lack of water. The slavers were very cruel

2 Africa
Slaves were captured by slavers and kept in slave forts until the slave ships arrived

slave fort

William Wilberforce, a rich friend of the Prime Minister, William Pitt, started a society in 1787 to abolish the slave trade. The plantation owners, who did not want to lose their cheap labour, fought this bitterly. However, Parliament slowly realised how horrible slavery was, and passed a law abolishing the British slave trade in 1807. Slavery in the British colonies was not abolished until 1833.

China teapot designed by Wedgwood

Homes

During the Industrial Revolution people moved from the countryside into the towns. The poor workers lived in tiny houses, often built by factory owners. The richer people lived in new, elegant terraced houses.

A Georgian kitchen

There was a 'dry cupboard' next to the fire for storing flour, salt, spices and tea

Houses had to be built in four styles or 'rates' by law. First rate houses were five storeys high and three windows wide. Fourth rate houses were three storeys high and two windows wide.

Ceilings were decorated with plaster mouldings. Walls were decorated with plaster panels

A first rate house

third floor servants' bedrooms

second floor bedrooms

first floor drawing room

ground floor

basement for cooking and stores

Large sash windows

coal hole

kitchen

ribbons and feathers in the hair

white lace cap

fan

long coat with high buttoned collar

knee breeches

buckled shoes

satin gown

A gentleman in the 1730s

white lace petticoats

Lady about 1780

What people wore

Georgian men's clothes became simpler and less colourful than the clothes of Stuart times. Gentlemen wore long coats with high collars that were usually worn open. Long waistcoats, knee length breeches, powdered wigs and three cornered hats were popular.

Hairstyles in the late 1700s could be very elaborate

high powdered wig on wire frame

Ladies wore full skirts and petticoats stretched over hoops. By the end of the period fashion had changed. Dresses were simpler and made of flimsy, see-through material like present day nightgowns. They had very high waistlines.

hat and coat based on French uniform

Ladies about 1810

silk bonnet

hair in ringlets

top hat

tail-coat with collar turned down

Some very rich friends of the Prince of Wales tried to outdo one another with extravagant clothes. They were called *dandies*

tight trousers

riding boots

By late Georgian times men wore clothes based on riding costume

The great Reform Act

In 1831 there were twenty four million people in Britain, yet only one man in fifty could vote, and no women.

Voters were given free lifts to the county towns to vote

Elections were very unfair. Voting was done in the open air and so voters could be bribed or bullied into voting a particular way.

Thugs were hired to threaten the voters

Bribery. One man spent £100,000 in entertainment and bribes and still lost the election

Voting areas were very unequal. In *rotten boroughs* like Old Sarum, half a dozen voters elected two MPs to Parliament. In *pocket boroughs* like Westbury, great landowners could make their tenants vote the way they wanted under threat of throwing them off the land. Thousands of people lived in new towns like Oldham, but had no MP at all.

People who did not vote or who were late were sometimes impersonated by someone else

Anyone allowed to vote was brought along even if they were mad

Many people demanded a reform of Parliament to make elections fairer. In the face of riots in parts of the country, Parliament passed the Reform Act. This removed most of the rotten boroughs and gave forty two large towns the right to have an MP. However, it gave the vote to only another 200,000 men. Though this was disappointing, it was the first step towards a fairer system.

The Press Gang

Britain only had a small army because, as an island, her real strength lay in the Royal Navy. The Navy guarded the British Isles and protected British trade routes abroad. However, life in the Navy was very hard and most men did not want to become sailors.

The press gang at work

Naval captains sent press gangs ashore to find sailors. Likely men were made drunk or knocked unconscious, then dragged on board. When naval ships visited a port, the men who lived there would often hide or run away, because they knew that once they were in the Navy they might never see their families again.

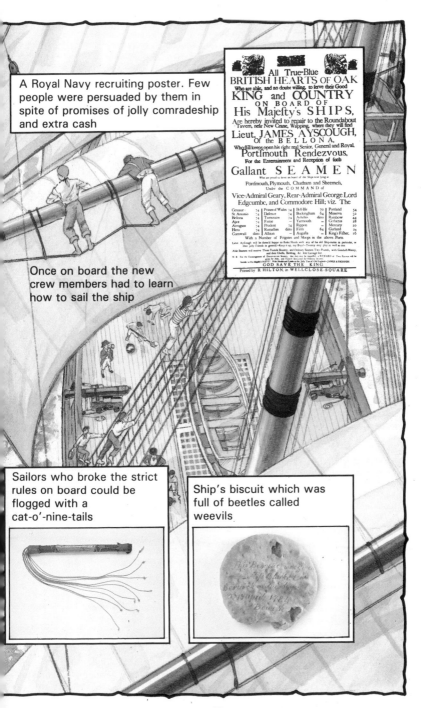

A Royal Navy recruiting poster. Few people were persuaded by them in spite of promises of jolly comradeship and extra cash

All True-Blue
BRITISH HEARTS OF OAK
Who are able, and no doubt willing, to ferve their Good
KING and COUNTRY
ON BOARD OF
His Majefty's SHIPS,
Are hereby invited to repair to the Roundabout
Tavern, near New Crane, Wapping, where they will find
Lieut. JAMES AYSCOUGH,
Of the BELLONA,
Who ftill keeps open his right real Senior, General and Royal,
Portfmouth Rendezvous,
For the Entertainment and Reception of fuch
Gallant SEAMEN
Who are proud to ferve on board of the Ships now lying at
Portfmouth, Plymouth, Chatham and Sheernefs,
Under the COMMAND of
Vice-Admiral Geary, Rear-Admiral George Lord
Edgcumbe, and Commodore Hill; viz. The

GOD SAVE THE KING
Printed by R HILTON in WELLCLOSE-SQUARE

Once on board the new crew members had to learn how to sail the ship

Sailors who broke the strict rules on board could be flogged with a cat-o'-nine-tails

Ship's biscuit which was full of beetles called weevils

Nelson's Column in Trafalgar Square commemorates the great sailor's victories over the French

The battle of Trafalgar

Nelson and Trafalgar

In 1805, the French emperor, Napoleon Bonaparte, had conquered most of Europe. He gathered a huge army at Boulogne and prepared to cross the Channel to invade Britain. Only the British fleet, led by Admiral Horatio Nelson, could save the country.

Nelson knew that if he could destroy the French fleet, the invasion barges would not dare to sail. He attacked the French navy off the coast of southern Spain near Cape Trafalgar. The battle was a great British victory and, although Nelson was killed, Napoleon had to call off his invasion.

The gundeck of Nelson's flagship, HMS *Victory*

The Duke of Wellington on his famous horse Copenhagen. He always seemed to be in the thick of the fighting. After his victory he was greeted in Britain as a national hero and later became Prime Minister.

Wellington and Waterloo

In 1815, Napoleon, who had been defeated by an alliance of Britain and the other European countries, escaped from his prison on the island of Elba off the west coast of Italy. When he reached France Napoleon quickly raised another army.

He attacked a small British army led by the Duke of Wellington near the village of Waterloo in Belgium. Wellington knew that if he held out until the Prussian army arrived, victory would be certain.

At Waterloo the British formed into squares and fired rapid *volleys* into the French *cavalry*. Not even Napoleon's famous Imperial Guard could break the British ranks.

Cavalry sword as used at Waterloo

After his defeat at Waterloo, Napoleon surrendered to the British. He was sent to the remote island of St Helena in the South Atlantic where he died.

ROMANS 700BC – AD383	SAXONS AND NORMANS 383 – 1272	MIDDLE AGES 1272 – 1485	TUDORS 1485 – 1603

1083 yrs ▷ 889 yrs ▷ 213 yrs ▷ 118 yrs ▷

TIMELINE GUIDE TO *A HISTORY OF BRITAIN*

How we know

The events in this book happened over two hundred years ago – so how do we know about them?

Historians use EVIDENCE, rather like detectives do, to piece a story together.

Many BOOKS and NEWSPAPERS describing Georgian times have survived to this day. Among the most famous novels are *Gulliver's Travels* and *Robinson Crusoe*. Plays like *She Stoops to Conquer* by Oliver Goldsmith also give an interesting picture of life then.

DEATH OF NELSON IN BATTLE

FRENCH FLEET DESTROYED

GLORIOUS VICTORY AT TRAFALGAR

London, Thursday, November 7, 1805.—*The London Gazette Extraordinary*, Wednesday, November 6. Dispatches, of which the following are copies, were received at the Admiralty this day

◀ Headlines from *The Times* newspaper announcing the victory at Trafalgar

There are still a lot of BUILDINGS that have also survived. A list of places to visit is on page 56.

50

The city of Bath has some of the best Georgian buildings in the country

Royal Circus, Bath

Archaeologists have EXCAVATED many Georgian sites and have reconstructed buildings at places like Ironbridge which was the first place where iron was made using coal.

OBJECTS found by archaeologists are often stored in museums. We have many objects that have survived from the Georgian Period.

There is a list of museums to visit on page 56.

Some of these old Georgian objects seem strange to us. What do you think this is? You will find the answer on page 56

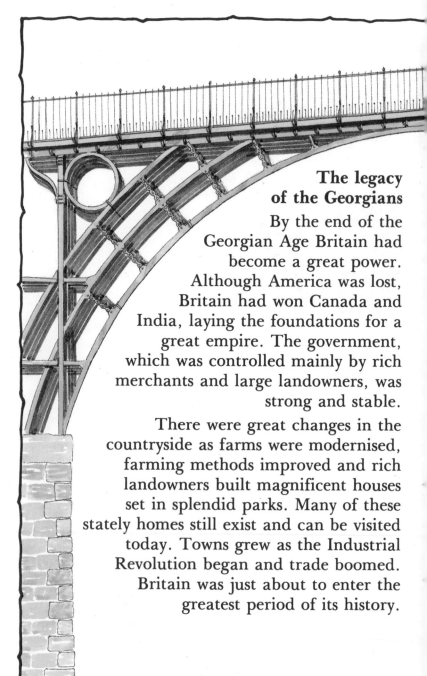

The legacy of the Georgians

By the end of the Georgian Age Britain had become a great power. Although America was lost, Britain had won Canada and India, laying the foundations for a great empire. The government, which was controlled mainly by rich merchants and large landowners, was strong and stable.

There were great changes in the countryside as farms were modernised, farming methods improved and rich landowners built magnificent houses set in splendid parks. Many of these stately homes still exist and can be visited today. Towns grew as the Industrial Revolution began and trade boomed. Britain was just about to enter the greatest period of its history.

the first iron bridge

steam engines

steamships

Stephenson's *Rocket*

factories

flush lavatories

gas lighting

balloons

buses

lightning conductors to protect buildings

Braille

revolver

oxygen and ammonia gases

OMNIBUS

Glossary

abolition: ending the slave trade

aborigines: the original inhabitants of Australia

anaesthetic: a gas which sends a patient to sleep during an operation

antiseptics: a liquid that stops wounds becoming infected

aqueduct: a bridge which carries a canal or water supply

auctioned: sold at a public sale to the highest bidder

bodysnatching: taking bodies from graves, usually for medical research

branded: marked with a red-hot iron

cabinet: a small group of ministers who form the policy of the government

cavalry: soldiers who fight on horseback

clan: a tribe of people who all have a common ancestor

colonists: people who settle in a foreign country

common: land on which villagers grazed their animals

convicts: criminals serving a sentence

cottagers: farm workers who lived in small houses on small plots of land

dandy: an elegant dresser

dissecting: cutting up bodies

empire: several foreign countries ruled by another country

fallow: uncultivated

fulling: washing wool

gout: a disease which causes painful swelling of small joints

Industrial Revolution: the changes that happen as a result of the coming of factories and powered machines

magistrate: an official who acts as judge in minor law cases

minister: a senior member of a government who has special responsibilities

molasses: a thick syrup made from sugar

pocket borough: a voting area owned by one person. The people in it could be persuaded to vote a particular way, or risk being thrown out of their houses

rotten borough: a voting area which sent a member to Parliament in spite of the fact that hardly anyone lived there

scurvy: a disease caused by lack of vitamin C

smelting: crushing and heating ore to extract the metal

strip: a piece of land farmed by a peasant

vaccinate: to protect a patient from a disease by giving them a small dose of a similar disease

volley: gunshots which are all fired at the same time

Index

Places to visit

Most city museums have collections of Georgian objects which are worth visiting. Derby, Stoke-on-Trent and Worcester Museums have fine pottery collections. Bath Museum of Costume and the Geffrye Museum, London, have excellent costume collections.

Gardens

Blenheim Palace, Oxfordshire
Castle Howard, Yorkshire
Petworth Park, Sussex
Stourhead, Wiltshire

Houses and buildings

Bath Pump Room, Avon
Buxton Assembly Room, Derbyshire
Castle Howard, Yorkshire
Charlotte Square, Edinburgh
Holkham Hall, Norfolk
John Wesley's House, City Road, London
Richmond Theatre, Yorkshire
Sugar merchant's house, Bristol
Theatre Royal, Bristol
Wilberforce's House, High Street, Hull

Museums

Cromford Mill, Derbyshire
Helmshore Higher Mill, Rossendale, Lancashire
Ironbridge Gorge Museum, Shropshire
Quarry Bank Mill, Cheshire
Science Museum, London
Victoria and Albert Museum, London

The object shown on page 51 is the first battery made by Alessandro Volta in 1800.